COUNTRIES

ISRAEL

R.L. Van

Big Buddy Books
An Imprint of Abdo Publishing
abdobooks.com

abdobooks.com

Published by Abdo Publishing, a division of ABDO, PO Box 398166, Minneapolis, Minnesota 55439. Copyright © 2023 by Abdo Consulting Group, Inc. International copyrights reserved in all countries. No part of this book may be reproduced in any form without written permission from the publisher. Big Buddy Books™ is a trademark and logo of Abdo Publishing.

Printed in the United States of America, North Mankato, Minnesota
102022
012023

THIS BOOK CONTAINS RECYCLED MATERIALS

Design: Emily O'Malley, Mighty Media, Inc.
Production: Mighty Media, Inc.
Editor: Jessica Rusick
Cover Photograph: Framalicious/Shutterstock Images
Interior Photographs: 0LANIA/Shutterstock Images, p. 30 (flag); AG-PHOTOS/Shutterstock Images, p. 27 (bottom); alefbet/Shutterstock Images, p. 26 (right); alvindom/Shutterstock Images, p. 7 (map); Barbarajo/Shutterstock Images, p. 15; Everett Collection/Shutterstock Images, p. 11; Framalicious/Shutterstock Images, p. 6 (top); Government Press Office/Wikimedia Commons, p. 28 (bottom); irisphoto1/Shutterstock Images, p. 25; jorisvo/Shutterstock Images, p. 9; Kathy Hutchins/Shutterstock Images, p. 23; Leonid Andronov/Shutterstock Images, p. 27 (top left); Levon Avagyan/Shutterstock Images, p. 17; lukulo/iStockphoto, pp. 5 (compass), 7 (compass); lunopark/Shutterstock Images, p. 30 (currency); Lunov Mykola/Shutterstock Images, p. 19; Max Topchii/Shutterstock Images, p. 27 (top right); Milner Moshe/Flickr, p. 21; Orlov Sergei/Shutterstock Images, p. 26 (left); Prachaya Roekdeethaweesab/Shutterstock Images, p. 28 (top left); Pyty/Shutterstock Images, p. 5 (map); Roman Yanushevsky/Shutterstock Images, p. 29 (top); Rostislav Ageev/Shutterstock Images, p. 6 (bottom); Sean Pavone/Shutterstock Images, p. 13; The White House/Wikimedia Commons, p. 29 (bottom); Wang An Qi/Shutterstock Images, p. 6 (middle); Wikimedia Commons, p. 28 (top right)
Design Elements: Mighty Media, Inc.
Country population and area figures taken from the CIA World Factbook

Library of Congress Control Number: 2022940502

Publisher's Cataloging-in-Publication Data
Names: Van, R.L., author.
Title: Israel / by R.L. Van
Description: Minneapolis, Minnesota : Abdo Publishing, 2023 | Series: Countries | Includes online resources and index.
Identifiers: ISBN 9781532199653 (lib. bdg.) | ISBN 9781098274856 (ebook)
Subjects: LCSH: Israel--Juvenile literature. | Middle East--Juvenile literature. | Asia--Juvenile literature. | Israel--History--Juvenile literature. | Geography--Juvenile literature.
Classification: DDC 915.694--dc23

CONTENTS

PASSPORT TO ISRAEL

Israel is in the Middle East. It is a small country on the Mediterranean Sea. About 8.9 million people live there.

DID YOU KNOW?

Hebrew and Arabic are the official languages of Israel. English is also commonly spoken there.

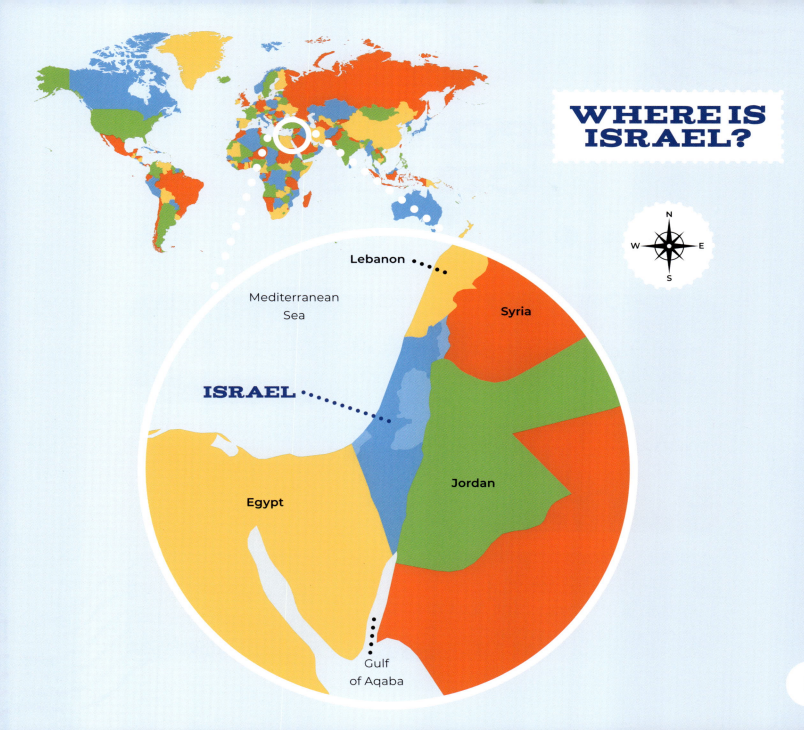

WHERE IS ISRAEL?

Lebanon

Mediterranean
Sea

Syria

ISRAEL

Jordan

Egypt

Gulf
of Aqaba

IMPORTANT CITIES

Jerusalem is Israel's **capital** and third-largest city. It is a historic and holy city with important religious sites.

Tel Aviv is Israel's largest city. It is a center of business and culture.

Haifa is Israel's second-largest city. It is an important port on the Mediterranean Sea.

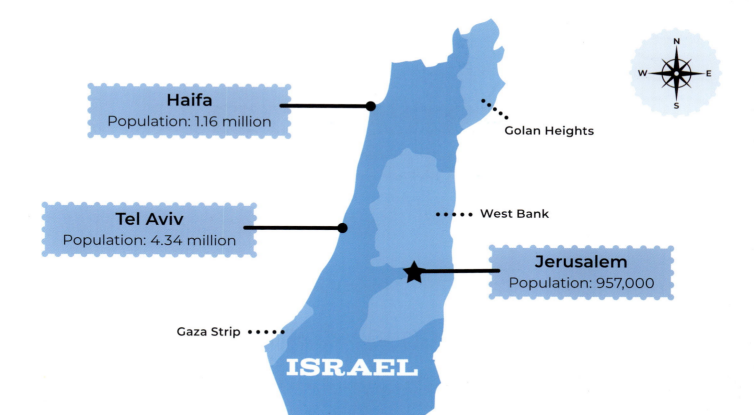

Haifa
Population: 1.16 million

Golan Heights

Tel Aviv
Population: 4.34 million

West Bank

Jerusalem
Population: 957,000

Gaza Strip

ISRAEL

DID YOU KNOW?

Tel Aviv's full name is Tel Aviv-Yafo. Most people just call it Tel Aviv.

SAY IT

Jerusalem
juh-ROO-suh-luhm

Tel Aviv
tehl uh-VEEV

Haifa
HEYE-fuh

7

ISRAEL IN HISTORY

Hebrew, or **Jewish**, people began settling in what is now Israel around 1500 BCE. The Kingdom of Israel formed around 1020 BCE. In 930 BCE, the kingdom broke apart. Over the next centuries, the land became known as Palestine. In the 600s, **Muslim** Arabs took it over.

King David (*left*) and his son King Solomon (*right*) made the Kingdom of Israel strong.

9

Muslim powers ruled Palestine for many years. In the late 1800s, **Jewish** people wanted to take back part of it. In 1948, part of Palestine became Israel. It was meant as a homeland for Jewish people. But Arabs in Palestine and nearby countries fought for this land. The fighting continues today.

DID YOU KNOW?

The Gaza Strip and the West Bank are **territories**. They are parts of Palestine that didn't become Israel.

Nearly 700,000 Jewish people immigrated to Israel between 1948 and 1951. Many had to stay in temporary shelters.

AN IMPORTANT SYMBOL

Israel's flag has blue stripes and a blue Star of David. The Star of David stands for **Judaism**.

Israel is a **parliamentary democracy**. The prime minister is head of government. The president is head of state. A group called the Knesset makes the country's laws.

The design of Israel's flag is based on a Jewish prayer shawl.

ACROSS THE LAND

Israel has plains, mountains, valleys, coasts, and deserts. Most people live near the Mediterranean Sea.

Bats, ibex, reptiles, hyenas, and many types of birds live in Israel. Evergreens, wildflowers, and fruit trees grow there.

Ibex are commonly spotted in Israel's Ein Gedi National Park.

EARNING A LIVING

Factory workers in Israel make electronics and medicines. Most Israelis have service jobs, such as working for the government.

Israel's **natural resources** include clay and fertilizer materials. Farmers grow citrus fruits, potatoes, and more. They raise cows and sheep.

Israel has a large diamond industry. Workers cut and polish diamonds using special tools.

LIFE IN ISRAEL

Most Israelis follow **Judaism**, though others follow **Islam**. People often eat foods such as hummus, falafel, and shawarma. Many people follow religious rules in their diets.

Most people in Israel live in cities. Sports are very popular there. Soccer and basketball are favorites.

Falafel is mashed, fried chickpeas. It is Israel's national dish.

FAMOUS FACES

• • • • • • • • • • • • •

Athlete Gal Fridman was born in Karkur, Israel. He started windsurfing when he was seven years old. In 2004, Fridman competed in the Summer Olympics in Athens, Greece. There, he won Israel's first-ever Olympic gold medal!

In 2005, Gal Fridman entered the International Jewish Sports Hall of Fame.

Gal Gadot was raised in Rosh Haayin, Israel. She became Miss Israel in 2004. Gadot is known for her work in the *Fast & Furious* movies. She also plays Wonder Woman. In 2018, Gadot was named one of *Time* magazine's 100 most influential people in the world.

Gal Gadot's martial arts skills helped her earn the role of Wonder Woman.

A GREAT COUNTRY

Israel has beautiful land and a rich history and culture. The people and places of Israel help make the world a more interesting place.

Mount Tabor is in northern Israel. It is a popular hiking spot. It is also an important religious site.

TOUR BOOK

If you ever visit Israel, here are some places to go and things to do!

SEE

Take a hike or ride a cable car to the top of the Masada fortress. The remains are about 2,000 years old!

EXPLORE

Visit the Jerusalem Biblical Zoo. It is home to many animals mentioned in the Bible.

DISCOVER

Climb the terraces and visit the Shrine of the Báb at the Bahá'i Gardens in Haifa.

SWIM

Float in the Dead Sea. The high salt content of the water allows you to float more easily!

PLAY

Glide down sand dunes in the Negev Desert, where you can go sandboarding!

TIMELINE

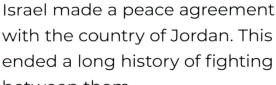

1948

Jewish people proclaimed the State of Israel. This started ongoing fights over the land.

1994

Israel made a peace agreement with the country of Jordan. This ended a long history of fighting between them.

1966

Israeli writer Shmuel Yosef Agnon won the Nobel Prize for Literature.

2010

A major forest fire destroyed parts of northern Israel.

2021

Violence between Israel and Palestine increased. People continued struggling for peace in the area.

2020

Leaders from Israel and other Arab countries signed the Abraham Accords at the White House. The accords helped normalize relations between the countries.

ISRAEL
UP CLOSE

Official Name
Medinat Yisra'el
(State of Israel)

Flag

Population
8,914,885 (2022 est.)
98th-most-populated country

Total Area
8,470 square miles
(21,937 sq km)
152nd-largest country

Official Languages
Hebrew, Arabic

Capital
Jerusalem

Currency
New Israeli shekel

Form of Government
Parliamentary
democracy

National Anthem
"Hatikvah"
("The Hope")

GLOSSARY

capital—a city where government leaders meet.

Islam—a religion based on a belief in Allah as God and Muhammad as his prophet.

Jewish—relating to the practice of Judaism or to the ancient Hebrews.

Judaism (JOO-dee-ih-zuhm)—a religion based on laws recorded in the Torah.

Muslim—a person who practices Islam.

natural resources—useful and valuable supplies from nature.

parliamentary democracy—a government in which the power is held by the people, who exercise it by voting. It is run by a legislature, which makes laws.

territories—areas that are not states but are under the authority of a country's government.

ONLINE RESOURCES

Booklinks
NONFICTION NETWORK
FREE! ONLINE NONFICTION RESOURCES

To learn more about Israel, please visit **abdobooklinks.com** or scan this QR code. These links are routinely monitored and updated to provide the most current information available.

INDEX